Live Action

Walking

Andrew Langley

Chrysalis Children's Books

First published in the UK in 2004 by
Chrysalis Children's Books
An imprint of Chrysalis Books Group PLC
The Chrysalis Building, Bramley Road, London W10 6SP

ISBN 1 84458 074 1

British Library Cataloguing in Publication Data for this book is available from the British Library.

Editorial Manager: Joyce Bentley
Project Editor: Clare Lewis

Produced by Bender Richardson White
Editor: Lionel Bender
Designer: Ben White
Production: Kim Richardson
Picture Researcher: Cathy Stastny

Printed in China

10 9 8 7 6 5 4 3 2 1

Words in **bold** can be found in Words to remember on page 31.

Picture credits
Corbis: 21 (Gallo Images), 27. Natural History Photo Agency: 19 (Ernie Janes). Digital Vision: 7, 9, 13. Rex Features Ltd: 4 (Stewart Cook), 12 (Henry T. Kaiser), 17 (Isopress), 20 (Alex Segre), 22 (Sipa), 23 (Palm Beach Post), 25 (Reso), 29 (Lehtikuva). RSPCA Photo Library: 11 (Mike Powles), 15 (Andrew Mounter). Steve Gorton: 1, 6, 8, 10, 14, 16, 18, 24, 26. Stockbyte: 28.
Cover: Corbis (main image, front inset centre left), Steve Gorton (back, front insets far left, far right), Digital Vision (front inset centre right). Illustration page 5: Jim Robins.

All reasonable care has been taken to ensure that activities
described are safe. The publisher shall not be liable for
any injuries caused by following instructions in this book.

Contents

Moving with muscles   4

Walking fast   6

Walking slowly   8

Creeping   10

Wading   12

Walking uphill   14

Going down   16

Walking tall   18

Pushing   20

Pulling   22

Single file   24

Walking a long way   26

Resting   28

Facts and figures   30

Words to remember   31

Index   32

Moving with muscles

To walk, you move your legs with a swinging action. You lift one foot at a time, so you always have the other foot on the ground.

'Walking the dog' is good **exercise** – for people and for dogs.

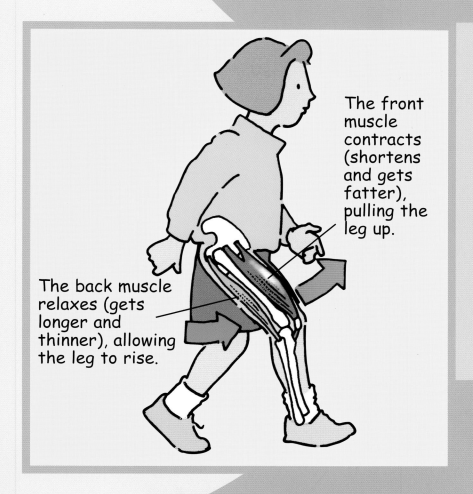

The front muscle contracts (shortens and gets fatter), pulling the leg up.

The back muscle relaxes (gets longer and thinner), allowing the leg to rise.

Muscles work in pairs. One muscle contracts while the other relaxes. In this way, muscles move the bones in your skeleton forward and back to help you to walk.

More than 20 pairs of muscles are used to walk.

You use **muscles** to make you walk. Muscles move the bones of your legs at the **joints**, such as your hips and knees.

Walking *fast*

To walk fast, take long strides – swing your legs far apart. Each foot lands on its heel and flattens. Then your toes act like springs to push you forwards.

Swinging your arms to and fro as you walk will help you move faster.

Elephants can walk at 15 kilometres an hour – faster than a person. They swing their long heavy trunks to help keep their balance as they move.

When an elephant walks, it always has at least one front leg and one hind leg on the ground at the same time.

An elephant has soft padded feet and makes very little noise when it walks.

Walking slowly

Sometimes you walk slowly. Perhaps you are tired, or you are carrying a heavy load of shopping. Or perhaps you are just not in a hurry.

People walk at a speed of about 6 kilometres an hour.

The wheels on a pram help you to push a load while you walk.

Tortoises and turtles walk very slowly. This is because they have a heavy shell to carry. Some walk at speeds of less than 250 metres an hour.

Turtles use their **paddles** to pull themselves over the ground.

Creeping

To creep up on someone, crouch down as low as you can. Take care not to make a noise when you put your feet down.

Get down to the ground as low as you can to make yourself difficult to see.

As soon as a tiger sees its **prey**, it crouches down and creeps forward. It keeps low so that it cannot be seen.

A tiger is hidden by long grass. When it gets close to its prey, it pounces.

When a tiger walks, its soft paws make no sound on the ground.

Wading

Walking through water is known as wading. Your muscles must work hard to push against the water.

If you put your feet down quickly, you will make a splash!

Flamingos have **webbed** feet that stop them from sinking into the mud.

Flamingos' long, thin legs look like matchsticks. The birds often stand on just one leg.

Flamingos wade in **shallow** lakes and rivers looking for food. They have long, thin legs that move easily through the water.

13

Walking uphill

Walking up a hill or stairs uses extra muscle power. As well as pushing you forwards, your legs have to push you upwards.

You use up more energy if you carry a load, such as a backpack, up hill.

To walk up to the top of the Empire State Building in New York you must climb 1576 steps.

The gecko can climb up walls and
window glass. It can even walk
upside down across the ceiling!

A gecko's feet have ridges with
millions of tiny hairs that help
the animal grip on surfaces.

Going down

Walk slowly and carefully down stairs or you can slip or trip over. Lean back a little to stop you from falling forwards.

Moving your arms will help you to keep your balance.

Squirrels can walk down or up the trunks of trees. They use the toes of their feet to grip the trunks and stop themselves falling.

When a squirrel walks down a tree, it uses its tail to help keep its balance.

Treecreepers are birds that walk down tree trunks.

17

Walking tall

To walk upright, keep your back straight.
You can 'walk tall' to see futher by
stretching your neck, back and legs,
and by moving on the tips of your toes.

Walking on **tiptoe**
raises your body so
you can see over
walls and fences.

Chimpanzees mostly walk on all fours. They will try to walk tall on their back legs when they want to scare off an enemy.

Most apes and monkeys live in trees. They use their arms to swing from branch to branch.

Chimpanzees can look very threatening, but they do not often attack other animals.

Pushing

Pushing a 'train' of trolleys is hard work. You have to use every muscle in your back, legs and arms.

Strong people can push along objects weighing more than three times their own weight.

Leaning forward helps your body push more in the right direction.

The scarab beetle pushes along balls of **dung**. The beetle stands on two of its legs and pushes with the other four.

Scarab beetles normally walk on all six legs.

Pulling

In a tug-of-war, two teams take hold of opposite ends of a rope and pull backwards. Each team tries to pull the other one towards it, using its weight and strength.

To win a tug-of-war, you have to pull the other team over a centre line.

Reindeer can pull heavy loads.
People use reindeer to pull
sledges across the snow.

Reindeer
have thick **fur**.
They can walk in
snow for hours
without getting
cold.

With their big **hooves**
and strong legs,
reindeer can walk in
deep snow.

Single file

People sometimes walk along in **single file** – one behind the other. The person in front decides where to go and how fast to walk. The others follow close behind.

Try marching in single file with everyone putting their left then right foot forward at the same time.

A long line of walking camels is called a 'caravan'.

Camels usually walk across deserts in single file. Adults go in the lead and at the back, with the young and their mothers inbetween.

Camels in a caravan often walk in step with each other.

Walking a long way

People enjoy walking long distances along coasts or over mountains. To do this you must be fit and healthy.

Long-distance walkers wear tough boots to help them to walk over all kinds of rocky and wet ground.

In the Olympic Games there are 20-kilometre and 50-kilometre walks. The 50-kilometre-race takes about 3 hr 45 min.

As a giraffe walks, its head and neck bob up and down. If it kept its neck stiff, it would soon get a neck ache!

Giraffes walk up to 30 kilometres a day to find food. They are so tall and have such big necks and bodies that their legs look too weak to support them – but they are not.

Resting

After a long walk, your leg muscles will feel tired and stiff. Your body will need a drink and food to replace the **energy** your muscles have used.

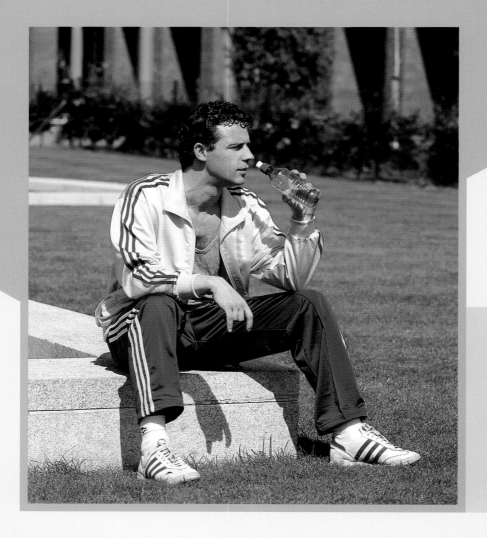

Once you sit down, your muscles will relax. Taking a cool drink will refresh you.

Animals need to rest after a long
walk. They sit down while their body
temperature cools down.

Dogs open their
mouths and pant with
their tongues
out to help them
cool down.

After exercise,
a person's or
animal's heartbeat
and breathing
slow. Sweating
helps cool the
body.

Facts and figures

The slowest mammal is the three-toed sloth of South America. It walks at just 0.16 kilometres an hour.

Some flies can taste with their feet. Blowflies can find out whether a food has sugar in it just by walking on it.

In a year, a caribou can walk more than 2250 kilometres across the Arctic, from south to north and back again.

The mudskipper - a fish that lives in central Africa - can stay out of water for several minutes 'walking' with its fins.

During an entire week (168 hours), a sloth spends only about 18 hours on the move – very slowly.

A lion usually walks about 10 kilometres a day in search of prey.

The longest distance ever walked on a tightrope is 1400 metres by Chinese athlete Ahdili in 2000. The rope was stretched between two mountain peaks.

The youngest ever holder of a world athletics record was a walker. China's Wang Yan was only 14 when she broke the record for the 50-kilometre walk.

Dung The droppings, or faeces, of animals.

Energy The power that lets us exercise and move our bodies.

Exercise Regular activity, for example walking, running and swimming. To do a sport or pastime that gets your muscles, lungs and heart working hard.

Fur The thick covering of hair on some animals' bodies.

Hoof The horny nail that grows over the lower part of some animals' feet.

Joint A part of the skeleton where two bones meet.

Muscle A bundle of elastic-like fibres that can tighten or relax to move parts of our bodies.

Paddle Flat part of the body that pushes against water when swimming.

Prey An animal that is hunted and caught for food.

Shallow Not very deep water along the banks of a river, lake or on the seashore.

Single file A single line of people or animals, one behind the other.

Tiptoe With the heel raised and only the toes and the ball of the foot touching the ground.

Webbed Wide, flat feet with stretches of skin between the toes.

Index

arms 6, 19, 20

balance 7, 17

creeping 10–11

energy 28

exercise 4, 29

foot, feet 4, 6, 7, 10, 12, 13, 15, 30

hoofs 23

joints 5, 11

legs 4, 5, 6, 7, 11, 13, 14, 16, 18, 19, 20, 21, 23, 27, 28

muscles 4, 5, 12, 14, 20, 28

pulling 22–23

pushing 20–21

single file 24–25

speed 8, 9

strides 6, 8

tiptoe 18

tired, tiring 8, 14, 28

toes 6, 17, 18

wading 12–13

walking a long way 26–27, 30

walking down 16–17

walking slowly 8–9

walking tall 18–19

walking up 14–15